KU-368-573

THE LAST YEARS OF BRITISH STEAM

Second Series

London
IAN ALLAN

TITLE PAGE: Class A4 No 60007 *Sir Nigel Gresley* leaves Edinburgh Waverley and passes through Princes St Gardens with 10.30 Edinburgh-Aberdeen on July 17, 1965.

BELOW: SR rebuilt 'West County' 4-6-2 No 34013, formerly named *Okehampton*, heads the last steam hauled 17:09 Waterloo-Salisbury commuter train through Winchfield cutting, running neck-and-neck with a Bournemouth electric mu, on June 9, 1967.

First published in magazine form 1972
Casebound edition first published 1973
Second impression 1974
Third impression 1977

ISBN 07110 0477 3

All rights reserved. No part of this book may be reproduced or transmitted in any form or by any means, electronic or mechanical, including photocopying, recording or by any information storage and retrieval system, without permission from the Publisher in writing.

© Ian Allan Ltd, 1973

Printed and published by
Ian Allan Ltd, Shepperton, Surrey.

The last years of British steam
2 / London Midland & Scottish

"Princess Coronation" Pacific No. 46233 *Duchess of Sutherland* emerges from Northchurch Tunnel, on the London outskirts, in May, 1958.
Photo by J. P. Mullett

Unrebuilt "Scot" No. 46100 *Royal Scot*, still carrying
commemorative American tour bell and nameplate at this date,
heads the 11.25 Euston-Birmingham near Bourne End, Herts,
in March, 1950.   *Photo by E. D. Bruton*

Pacific No. 46225 *Duchess of Gloucester* pulls out of Penrith
with a Keswick-Crewe and Manchester through train in
August, 1964.
                                        Photo by Derek Cross

ABOVE: A pair of Class 9 2-10-0s toil up the "Long Drag" of the Settle-Carlisle main line near Selside with a track train in August, 1967. *Photo by E. F. Bentley*

LEFT: Another Class 9 2-10-0, No. 92249, at grips with the final stretch of 1 in 100 to Ais Gill summit with an up mineral train on the Carlisle-Leeds main line in April, 1967. In the background is Wild Boar Fell. *Photo by T. Worsley*

ABOVE RIGHT: No. 92022, a Crosti-boilered Class 9 2-10-0 as built with rear-boilerside exhaust, drifts through Mill Hill, in the London suburbs, with Midland line coal in September, 1955. *Photo by C. D. D. Newton*

RIGHT: A Crosti-boilered 2-10-0 after modification to orthodox exhaust arrangement—No. 92022 in September, 1964 on the North Western main line heading up freight for London into Northchurch Tunnel. *Photo by Brian Stephenson*

LEFT: Tanks gather at Bangor in June, 1963—from left to right: the front end of Class 2 2-6-2T No. 41226 on an Amlwch train; Class 4 2-6-4Ts Nos. 42478 and 42074 on a Butlins Camp special from Pwllheli; and Class 4 2-6-4T No. 42488 on a Chester parcels. *Photo by N.Kneale*

BELOW: Bangor again, in September, 1958. Left is "Jubilee" No. 45629 *Straits Settlements* on a Holyhead train; centre, standard Class 4 2-6-4T No. 80095 on a Pwllheli train and right Class 4 2-6-4T No. 42478 in the yard. *Photo by I. J. McIntosh*

RIGHT: The "Cambrian Radio Cruise Train", including an ex-Midland and ex-"Coronation Scot" saloon, on the North Wales coast at Penmaenmawr sands behind standard Class 4 4-6-0 No. 75033. *Photo by K. Field*

BELOW RIGHT: BR standard Class 5 4-6-0 No. 73070 pulls out of Colwyn Bay with the 11.30 Llandudno Junction-Chester in September, 1957. *Photo by K. L. Cook*

ABOVE: Rebuilt "Patriot" 4-6-0 No. 45512 *Bunsen* storms out of Carlisle with a Preston-bound football special on a February Saturday in 1964. On the right is Class 5 4-6-0 No. 44671.

Photo by A. R. Thompson

BELOW: Unrebuilt "Patriot" 4-6-0 No. 45544 heads a Euston-Manchester express near Hanslope, Bucks in June, 1954.

Photo by P. Hutchinson

TOP LEFT: Compound 4-4-0 No. 41083 waits to leave Birmingham New Street with the 17.45 stopping train to Bristol in April, 1958; on the right is sister engine No. 40931.   *Photo by M. Mensing*

LEFT: A pair of compound 4-4-0s, Nos. 41063 and 41100, en route from Stockport to Crewe with the Ian Allan *Trains Illustrated* "Pennine Limited" railtour special of April, 1958.
    Photo by R. J. Blenkinsop

ABOVE: Class 2P 4-4-0 No. 40580 leaves Stafford with the 17.50 stopping train to Crewe in the 1950s.
    Photo by B. E. Morrison

RIGHT: Class 3P 4-4-0 No. 40728 double-heads "Jubilee" 4-6-0 No. 45682 *Trafalgar* on the 7.40 Bristol-Newcastle at Derby in August, 1950.
    Photo by R. J. Buckley

ABOVE: "Jubilee" 4-6-0 No. 45629 *Straits Settlements* attacks
the gradient near Shap Wells with a Birmingham-Edinburgh train.
Photo by Derek Cross

ABOVE LEFT: "Britannia" Pacific No. 70012 rounds the castle
walls at Conway with a down North Wales coast extra in June, 1966.
Photo by W. Brian Alexander

LEFT: BR standard Class 6 4-6-2 No. 72008 *Clan Macleod*
re-starts the 13.26 Carlisle-Perth from Gleneagles in September,
1964.   *Photo by W. J. V. Anderson*

LEFT: A Class 4F 0-6-0 pounds up the Lickey Incline with empty wagons from the West in January, 1958.

Photo by F. A. Haynes

RIGHT: Class 4F 0-6-0s Nos. 44015 and 44175 leave Stratford-on-Avon for Broom Junction on the ex-SMJ line with coal in January, 1956.

Photo by T. E. Williams

BELOW: Up freight near Walton, south of Wakefield, behind Class 4F 0-6-0 No. 44345 in December 1963.

Photo by D. Ian Wood

BELOW: During its period of "working" preservation the
ex-Highland Railway "Jones Goods" 4-6-0 No. 103 heads a special
away from Greenock Princes Pier past Port Glasgow in March,
1965.   *Photo by W. J. V. Anderson*

RIGHT: Ex-Caledonian 0-6-0 No. 57568 ambles through
the hills near Abington with the Carstairs-Lockerbie pick-up freight
on the West Coast main line.   *Photo by Derek Cross*

BELOW RIGHT: Highland line coal on the climb from
Aviemore to Slochd summit behind Pickersgill 4-4-0 No. 54482 and
a Class 5 4-6-0 in August, 1959.   *Photo by W. J. V. Anderson*

LEFT: Headed by an Ivatt Class 2 2-6-0 a special leaves Keswick for Penrith on an August evening in 1965.
Photo by W. J. V. Anderson

BELOW LEFT: BR standard Class 2 2-6-2T No. 84005 sets off from Seaton with the 17.57 to Stamford on a May afternoon in 1964. *Photo by G. D. King*

RIGHT: An Ivatt Class 2 2-6-0 banks a ballast train out of Manchester Victoria in April, 1967. *Photo by S. M. Hammond*

BELOW: Ivatt Class 4 2-6-0 No. 43002 makes for the Erewash Valley line out of Trent in February, 1966.
Photo by G. D. King

ABOVE: Ex-Caledonian 0-4-4T No. 55224 skirts Loch Leven
with the afternoon Ballachulish-Oban train in August, 1961.

Photo by S. C. Crook

BELOW: London Tilbury & Southend Railway centenary day,
March 3, 1956—restored LTS 4-4-2T No. 80 *Thundersley*
leaves Southend Central for London with a celebration special,
passing sister engine No. 41946.

Photo by S. Creer

ABOVE: Ex-Midland 0-4-4T No. 58038 at Romford on the
Upminster push-pull in September, 1949.   *Photo by R. E. Vincent*

BELOW: A special from Broughton to Edinburgh near Biggar
behind ex-Caledonian 0-4-4T No. 55124 in September, 1961.
Photo by Derek Cross

LEFT: Single-line working because of trouble in Dove Holes Tunnel on a January Saturday in 1968; Stanier 2-8-0 No. 48192 restarts a freight at Chinley South Junction after crossing to the wrong line, while No. 48775 on another freight waits to follow.

Photo by D. E. Gouldthorp

RIGHT: Single line token exchange on the Highland between the Etteridge crossing keeper near Newtonmore and the crew of Class 3F 0-6-0 No. 57575.

Photo by Alex Coupar

BELOW: A Manchester-Leeds Copley Hill freight drifts through Marsden behind ex-LNW 0-8-0 No. 49119. *Photo by K. Field*

LEFT: "Jubilee" 4-6-0 No. 45647 *Sturdee* climbs to Standedge Tunnel with the 9.15 Leeds-Llandudno in August, 1966.
Photo by M. Pope

BOTTOM LEFT: "Patriot" 4-6-0 No. 45539 *E. C. Trench* at Manchester Exchange on a Brindle Heath-Miles Platting freight in August, 1961.
Photo by J. R. Carter

BELOW: Pacific No. 46230 *Duchess of Buccleuch* heads for Glasgow near Lamington with the 10.15 from Euston in September, 1961.
Photo by Derek Cross

ABOVE: "Britannia" Pacific No. 70015 *Apollo* tops Grayrigg
bank with the 4.28 Carlisle-Manchester parcels on a July morning
in 1967.   *Photo by J. H. Cooper-Smith*

ABOVE LEFT: "Britannia" Pacific No. 70013 *Oliver Cromwell*
storms out of Preston with a Carlisle-Blackpool football special
on Boxing Day, 1967.   *Photo by R. J. Clarke*

LEFT: Fowler 2-6-4T No. 42365 simmers at Buxton NW
awaiting 19.30 departure for Manchester on a July evening in 1955.
                                              Photo by J. F. Oxley

ABOVE: A Caprotti valve gear BR standard Class 5 4-6-0 crosses the Tay at Perth with an evening Glasgow-Dundee train in July, 1964.   *Photo by W. J. V. Anderson*

BELOW: Class 6 4-6-2 No. 72006 *Clan Mackenzie* heads north from Carlisle.   *Photo by Ronald Wright*

ABOVE: "Jubilee" 4-6-0 No. 45675 *Hardy* makes for the east out of Carnforth on the Furness and Midland line with a parcels train in June, 1966.   *Photo by B. J. Ashworth*

BELOW: BR standard Class 4 2-6-0 No. 76096 starts a Heads of Ayr-Edinburgh holiday camp train out of Ayr in June, 1965.
                                                        Photo by Derek Cross

RIGHT: Class 8F 2-8-0 No. 48410 hauls coal up to Copy Pit summit, Lancs.
Photo by K. P. Lawrence

BELOW: Another scene on the Copy Pit climb—Class WD 2-8-0 No. 90656 attacks the 1 in 68 out of Todmorden with coal from the West Riding to Rose Grove, Burnley in July, 1964.
Photo by D. Ian Wood

BOTTOM RIGHT: Class WD 2-8-0 No. 90588 and Stanier 2-8-0 No. 48225 toil up to Standedge Tunnel near Golcar with a 20 coach rake of Leeds-Manchester empty stock in September, 1963.
Photo by G. W. Morrison

BELOW: "Princess Royal" 4-6-2
No. 46209 *Princess Beatrice* on the last stage
of the climb to Shap summit with a
Euston-Glasgow express in August, 1960.
Photo by P. H. Groom

RIGHT: A Class 5 4-6-0 pilots Pacific
No. 46247 *City of Liverpool* through
Winwick, near Warrington, on a Glasgow-
Birmingham express in March, 1962
Photo by J. R. Carter

BOTTOM RIGHT: Class 5 4-6-0
No. 44736 on a Blackpool-Grangemouth
holiday relief in July, 1963; photographed
south of Tebay.   *Photo by Derek Cross*

LEFT: Class 2 2-6-0s Nos. 46458 and 46434 about to double-head a Keswick special out of Carlisle in August, 1964.
Photo by A. R. Thompson

BELOW:Class 2 4-4-0 No. 40411 heads an up Midland line stopping train away from Wing Tunnel in September, 1956.
Photo by P. H. Wells

RIGHT: Ex-Highland "Clan Goods" 4-6-0 No. 57954 moves freight out of Forres.
Photo by W. J. V. Anderson

BELOW RIGHT: BR standard Class 4 4-6-0s Nos. 75019 and 75027 double-head a special out of Hellifield towards Skipton in July, 1968.
Photo by L. A. Nixon

ABOVE: Ex-Somerset & Dorset 2-8-0 No. 53807 pilots a Class 4F
0-6-0 out of Evercreech Junction en route for Bath with a
special in June, 1964.   *Photo by M. Pope*

ABOVE: Beyer-Garratt No. 47979 wheels freight through
Stamford Town in January, 1953.   *Photo by P. H. Wells*

BELOW: Ex-LNW 0-8-0 No. 49344 approaches Tile Hill, on the
Coventry-Birmingham main line, with down freight in
March, 1959.   *Photo by M. Mensing*

ABOVE: Class J94 0-6-0STs Nos. 68006 and 68012 take a run at Hopton Incline with a Cromford & High Peak enthusiasts' brake-van special in April, 1967. *Photo by J. R. Hillier*

BELOW: Another Cromford & High Peak memory—a J94 0-6-0ST at Middleton Top. *Photo by C. T. Gifford*

ABOVE: A Class 2-6-4T crosses Whalley Arches with the
19.29 Blackburn-Hellifield in May, 1961. *Photo by K. Roberts*

BELOW: A Fairburn 2-6-4T banks freight up Shap in
March, 1967. *Photo by B. Stephenson*

LEFT: BR standard Class 5 4-6-0 No. 73054 pauses at Birmingham New Street in November, 1957.
Photo by M. Mensing

BOTTOM LEFT: BR standard Class 4 4-6-0 No. 75019 heads the last Skipton-Barnoldswick pick-up freight on July 29, 1966.
Photo by M. Mitchell

RIGHT: Class 4 2-6-0 No. 43029 climbs Shap with a local freight in August, 1966.
Photo by J. Clarke

BELOW: Stanier 2-6-0 No. 42948 accelerates a southbound goods out of Penrith in August, 1964.
Photo by Derek Cross

LEFT: "Jubilee" class 4-6-0 No. 45626 *Seychelles* re-starts
a Newcastle-Bristol express from Derby in August, 1959.
Photo by J. Cupit

BELOW LEFT: "Crab" 2-6-0 No. 42823 leaves Bulwell Market
with a Skegness special in August, 1959.   *Photo by T. G. Hepburn*

BELOW: A southbound Carlisle-Leeds freight coasts through
Gargrave behind a Class WD 2-8-0 in September, 1965.
Photo by J. R. Hillier

BELOW: Stanier three-cylinder 2-6-4T
No. 42531 leaves Benfleet with a Fenchurch
Street-Shoeburyness train in July, 1960.
Photo by Frank Church

BELOW: Class 3 2-6-2T No. 40151
heads the 9.55 Muirkirk-Edinburgh out of
Happendon, passing ex-Caledonian 0-6-0
No. 57386 on the Muirkirk-Lanark goods.
Photo by Derek Cross

Peterborough East in June, 1960 with Fowler 2-6-4T No. 42353 on the 12.40 (ABOVE) and Stanier 2-6-4T No. 42478 on the 18.00 to Wellingborough and Northampton. *Photos by M. Mensing*

LEFT: A Class 9F 2-10-0 near Barnston with an ore train for John Summers ironworks at Shotton, photographed in October, 1967. *Photo by R. I. Vallance*

RIGHT: Ex-Lancashire & Yorkshire 0-6-0s Nos. 52390 and 52328 wait for their next banking duty at Manchester Victoria. *Photo by K. Field*

BELOW: Class 3F 0-6-0 No. 43638 passes Bredbury with Manchester-bound freight. *Photo by K. Field*

BOTTOM: Midland Class 1F 0-6-0T No. 41739 shunts at Staveley in March, 1961. *Photo by J. P. Mullett*

ABOVE: Freight for Buxton disappears towards Chinley North Junction behind Class 8F 2-8-0 No. 48744 in April, 1967.
Photo by J. R. Hillier

LEFT: Class 2 4-4-0 No. 40540 starts the 12.12 local for Nottingham out of Derby in May, 1950. *Photo by R. J. Buckley*

The last years of British steam

3/ Eastern, North Eastern & Scottish Regions

RIGHT: A Class 9F 2-10-0 banks a Tyne Dock-Consett ore train through Beamish.
Photo by M. Dunnett

LEFT: Class A3 4-6-2 No. 60087 *Blenheim* emerges from the Mound Tunnel, Edinburgh, with an Aberdeen express in September, 1957.

Photo by P. H. Groom

RIGHT UPPER: Class V2 2-6-2 No. 60982 at York with the 10.08 to Bournemouth in April, 1963.

Photo by J. M. Rayner

RIGHT LOWER: The Sunday 10.00 to Kirkcaldy leaves Glasgow Queen Street behind Class B1 4-6-0 No. 61342 in October, 1960.

Photo by S. Rickard

ABOVE LEFT: Class J17 0-6-0 No. 65530 moves local freight out of Kings Lynn in July, 1959. *Photo by P. H. Wells*

ABOVE RIGHT: Class J15 0-6-0 No. 65445 near Long Melford with the Saturday 13.22 Cambridge-Colchester in July, 1958. *Photo by G. R. Mortimer*

BELOW LEFT: Another J15, No. 65476, climbs out of Ongar with an enthusiasts' excursion over GE lines in April, 1962. *Photo by A. R. Butcher*

BELOW RIGHT: Class F5 2-4-2T No. 67217 at Langford & Ulting Halt with the 8.50 Witham-Maldon in July, 1953. *Photo by G. R. Mortimer*

LEFT: Class A2 4-6-2 No. 60532 *Blue Peter* restarts the 13.30 Aberdeen-Glasgow out of Forfar in July, 1966.   *Photo by J. Taylor*

ABOVE: "Britannia" Pacific No. 70041 *Sir John Moore* speeds through Sandy with the 16.12 Kings Cross-Grimsby and Cleethorpes in August, 1961.   *Photo by M. Mensing*

BELOW: Another memory of Sandy in August, 1961—Class A2/3 4-6-2 No. 60516 *Hycilla* heads for London with the 12.20 Hull-Kings Cross.   *Photo by M. Mensing*

ABOVE: Class J2 0-6-0 No. 65016 pulls out of Boston with a Nottingham Victoria-Mablethorpe through train in April, 1952.

Photo by P. J. Lynch

BELOW: Class J6 0-6-0 No. 64180 nears Woodhall Junction with a pick-up goods from Lincoln in April, 1953. *Photo by J. F. Oxley*

ABOVE: Class N2 0-6-2T No. 69521 shunts
vans at Peterborough North in June, 1960.
Photo by M. Mensing

BELOW: A Class J52 0-6-0ST lifts a freight
over the Harringay flyover, London, in
October, 1957.   *Photo by S. Creer*

LEFT: Class O2/3 2-8-0 No. 63937 between Hampole and Carcroft with southbound coal in February, 1962.   *Photo by M. Mitchell*

RIGHT: Class O4/3 2-8-0 No. 63859 makes for Stanton Ironworks past Bagthorpe Junction, Nottingham, with ore in June, 1963.
                                        Photo by T. Boustead

BELOW LEFT: A Colwick-Stanton ore train between Nuthall and Kimberley on the ex-GN line in September, 1963, headed by Class O4/8 2-8-0 No. 63816.   *Photo by T. Boustead*

BELOW RIGHT: Class O4/7 2-8-0 No. 63770 heads an up coal train from the Pinxton branch on to the Nottingham-Derby Friargate line at Answorth Junction in August, 1964.
                                        Photo by T. Boustead

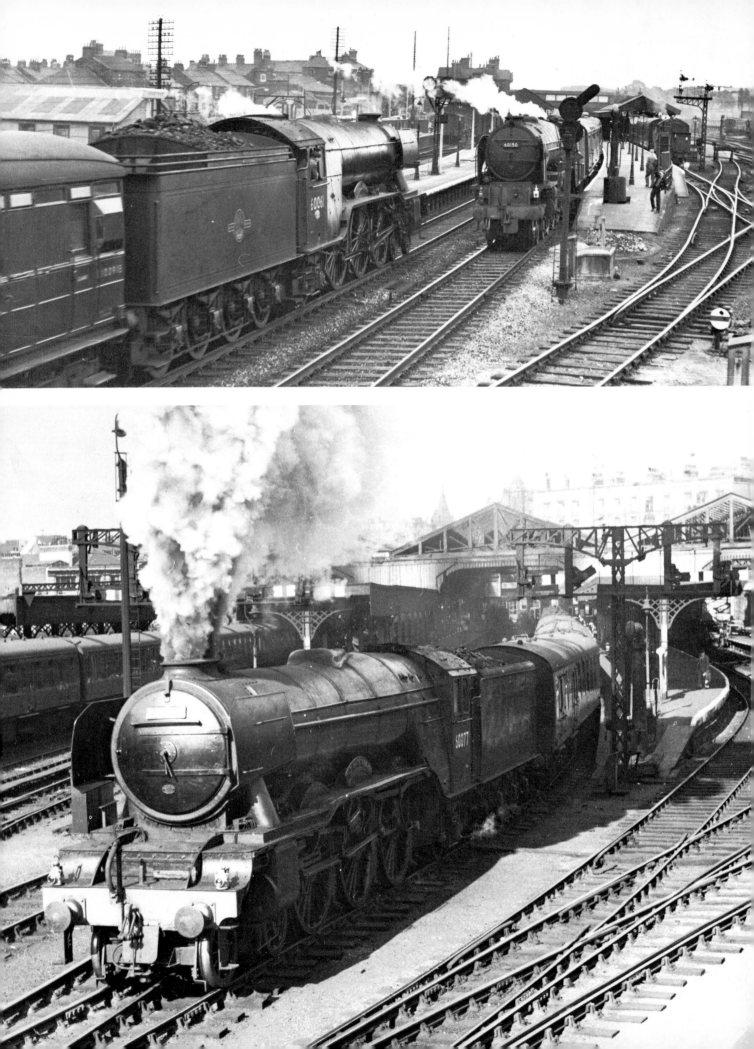

FAR LEFT: Class A3 4-6-2 No. 60061 *Pretty Polly* brings a Newcastle-Kings Cross train into Grantham, where Class A1 4-6-2 No. 60150 *Willbrook* stands at the platform with the down "Scarborough Flyer" in August, 1962. *Photo by J. M. Rayner*

LEFT: Class A4 4-6-2 No. 60009 *Union of South Africa* takes water at Perth in July, 1964. *Photo by E. Oldham*

BELOW LEFT: Class A3 4-6-2 No. 60077 *The White Knight* loses its feet as it starts the 17.30 for Kings Cross out of Leeds Central in September, 1961. *Photo by J. M. Rayner*

BELOW: A down fitted freight north of Darlington behind Class A1 4-6-2 No. 60140 *Balmoral* in October, 1964. *Photo by J. E. Hoggarth*

ABOVE LEFT: Class V2 2-6-2 No. 60939 attacks the 1 in 100 through
How Gill with the 9.38 Carlisle-Newcastle Tyne Yard freight in October,
1964.   *Photo by P. J. Robinson*

BELOW LEFT: The unique Class V2 with smoke deflectors, No. 60813,
leaves Dundee with the 14.50 Perth goods in August, 1966.
                                                        Photo by S. C. Crook

ABOVE RIGHT: No. 60836 storms out of Aberdeen past Cove Bay on a
"last V2" special trip in November, 1966.   *Photo by P. Riley*

ABOVE LEFT: Winter's day study of a Class A8 4-6-2T on the Hull-Scarborough line.
Photo by S. E. Teasdale

ABOVE RIGHT: Class B16/1 4-6-0 No. 61410 trundles a freight up the Darlington-York main line near Beningbrough in June, 1954.
Photo by P. Ransome-Wallis

BELOW LEFT: Class D49/1 4-4-0 No. 62723 *Nottinghamshire* ready to leave Scarborough with the 11.30 for Hull in July, 1958.
Photo by M. Mensing

BELOW RIGHT: Class D49/2 4-4-0 No. 62745 *The Hurworth* pilots Class WD 2-8-0 No. 90273 near Harrogate on a southbound freight in May, 1955.

ABOVE: Class D16/3 4-4-0 No. 62580 awaits the right-away from Norwich Thorpe with the 17.35 to Swaffham in September, 1954.
Photo by R. E. Vincent

BELOW: Class D40 4-4-0 No. 62267 leaves Aviemore with an evening freight for Boat of Garten in August, 1953. *Photo by J. L. Stevenson*

ABOVE: Class E4 2-4-0 No. 62789 at Beccles
with the 15.25 to Tivetshall in September, 1952.
Photo by R. E. Vincent

BELOW: The 16.35 Glasgow-Perth near
Mawcarse behind Class D11 4-4-0 No. 62672
Baron of Bradwardine in September, 1956.
Photo by W. J. V. Anderson

ABOVE: Class B12/3 4-6-0 No. 61549 ambles away from Shenfield with an up parcels in June, 1954.   *Photo by B. E. Morrison*

LEFT: Class B17/4 4-6-0 No. 61657 *Doncaster Rovers* moves the 18.35 Leicester-Peterborough out of Syston in April, 1960.

Photo by G. D. King

RIGHT: Class B2 4-6-0 No. 61644 *Earlham Hall* heads the 16.57 Cambridge express out of Liverpool Street in April, 1951.

Photo by J. R. Eagles

BELOW: Class D16/3 4-4-0 No. 62568 arrives at Leicester with the 12.52 from Peterborough East in November, 1955. *Photo by P. H. Wells*

LEFT: Class Q6 0-8-0 No. 63395 accelerates a coal train for Sunderland South Dock past Hall Dene Crossing in July, 1967.
Photo by D. E. Gouldthorp

ABOVE: A pair of Q6 0-8-0s attack the climb out of Stella Gill with coal for Consett.
Photo by Verdun Wake

BELOW: Class J27 0-6-0 No. 65872 at Tyne Dock in October, 1966. *Photo by M. Dunnett*

TOP: Class A4 4-6-2 No. 60027 *Merlin* leaves Aberdeen with the 17.15 to Glasgow in May, 1964.
Photo by W. J. V. Anderson

RIGHT: Class A3 4-6-2 No. 60063 *Isinglass* at Kings Cross in March, 1963.
Photo by Brian Stephenson

ABOVE: Class A1 4-6-2 No. 60138 *Boswell* pauses at York with the up "Heart of Midlothian".

ABOVE: Class K3 2-6-0 No. 61928 and Class A3 4-6-2 No. 60097 *Humorist* double-head an Edinburgh express out of Aberdeen in August, 1952. *Photo by S. E. Teasdale*

LEFT: Class K2 2-6-0 No. 61760 brings freight into Boston, passing Class J69 0-6-0 No. 68543, in October, 1954. *Photo L. Perrin*

RIGHT: Class K1 2-6-0 No. 62021 leaves
Alnwick with the 17.55 to Alnmouth in May,
1966.   *Photo by M. S. Burns*

BELOW: Class K2 2-6-0s Nos. 61794 *Loch Oich*
and 61785 on the Glenfinnan climb with a Fort
William-Mallaig train in August, 1954.
                    Photo by W. J. V. Anderson

RIGHT: Class A1 4-6-2 No. 60155 *Borderer* heads a down freight out of York in April, 1965.   *Photo by J. D. Benson*

FAR RIGHT: Class A3 4-6-2 No. 60035 *Windsor Lad* climbs to Glenfarg with the 12.5 Perth-Edinburgh in January, 1961.
    Photo by W. J. V. Anderson

RIGHT BELOW: A Dundee-Perth train near Glencarse in August, 1966 behind Class A2 4-6-2 No. 60530 *Sayajirao*.
    Photo by S. C. Crook

ABOVE LEFT: Class D20 4-4-0 No. 62395 moves the 11.2 stopping train
to York out of Doncaster in May, 1955.   *Photo by P. J. Lynch*

ABOVE RIGHT: During its period of active preservation in North British
livery Class D34 4-4-0 No. 256 (former NBR number) *Glen Douglas* heads
a local train out of Dunfermline Lower in March, 1962.
                                                    Photo by W. J. V. Anderson

BELOW LEFT: A Rosyth Dockyard-Cardenden workman's train passes
Inverkeithing behind Class D30 4-4-0 No. 62418 *The Pirate* in April, 1959.
                                                    Photo by S. C. Crook

LEFT: A Class N5 0-6-2T and WD 2-8-0 at Langwith Junction.

ABOVE: Class C13 4-4-2T No. 67401 leaves Guide Bridge sidings, Manchester, with a local train in November, 1951.

TOP RIGHT: Class A5 4-6-2T No. 69818 heads a staff train out of Bulwell Common for Holinwell in October, 1958.

CENTRE RIGHT: Class D11 4-4-0 No. 62661 *Gerard Powys Dewhurst* arrives at Northwich with the 12.52 from Chester in August, 1955, stopping alongside Class 2 2-6-2T No. 41229 on the 12.38 to Crewe.

BOTTOM RIGHT: Class J11 0-6-0 No. 64380 eases a local out of Retford on to the Sheffield line in June, 1953.
*Photos by J. Cupit, T. Lewis, D. Swale,
B. E. Morrison, J. P. Wilson*

TOP RIGHT: Class A3 4-6-2 No. 60054 *Prince of Wales* heads the Sunday 14.15 Kings Cross-Edinburgh near Markham in June, 1958.
Photo by T. Lewis

ABOVE: The "Yorkshire Pullman" emerges from Ardsley Tunnel behind Class A1 4-6-2 No. 60134 *Foxhunter*.
Photo by K. Field

BOTTOM RIGHT: Class A4 4-6-2 No. 60024 *Kingfisher* storms out of Gleneagles with the Aberdeen-Glasgow "Grampian" in August, 1965.
Photo by S. C. Crook

ABOVE: Class J36 0-6-0 No. 65248 passes a J37 and skirts Portobello yard with a freight from Leith for the Edinburgh freight loop in July, 1953.   *Photo by P. H. Wells*

LEFT: Class N15 0-6-2T No. 69181 and Class D34 4-4-0 No. 62496 *Glen Loy* simmer between jobs at Cowlairs in March, 1961.
                                     Photo by S. Rickard

BELOW: Class J38 0-6-0 No. 65930 on the Loch Ore causeway with coal from Mary colliery for Kelty in March, 1966.
                            Photo by W. J. V. Anderson

TOP RIGHT: A Class J37 0-6-0 leaves Leslie, Fife, with freight in June, 1965.
                            Photo by W. J. V. Anderson

BOTTOM RIGHT: Privately-owned and preserved, Class K4 2-6-0 No. 3442 *The Great Marquess* crosses Newton Gap Viaduct on the Bishop Auckland-Durham line with a special in April, 1965.   *Photo by J. Lummas*

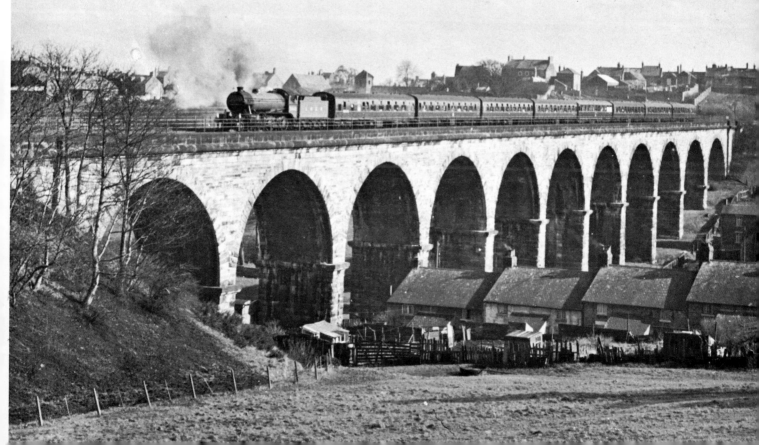

ABOVE LEFT: Class WD 2-8-0 No. 90321 passes Boldon Colliery with Gateshead-Sunderland empties in January, 1967.
Photo by M. Dunnett

ABOVE RIGHT: Class 9F 2-10-0 No. 92065 climbs out of South Pelaw with freight for Consett in September, 1966.
Photo by M. Dunnett

BELOW LEFT: Class J52 0-6-0ST No. 68888 emerges from Copenhagen Tunnel with a transfer freight from Kings Cross yard on a July morning in 1953. *Photo by A. R. Carpenter*

BELOW RIGHT: A Class Q6 0-8-0 en route for Consett with steel empties passes Stella Gill in 1965.
Photo by M. Dunnett

ABOVE: Class C16 4-4-2T No. 67484 moves a
local away from Dundee Tay Bridge in April,
1953.   *Photo by J. Robertson*

BELOW: The 11.15 to Stirling leaves
Inverkeithing behind Class V3 2-6-2T No. 67669
in February, 1960.   *Photo by W. A. C. Smith*

ABOVE: Saffron Walden in July, 1954, with the Audley End branch train waiting behind Class G5 0-4-4T No. 67269.

Photo by G. M. Staddon

BELOW: Class L1 2-6-4T No. 67758 pauses at Ashby Magna with the 17.30 Nottingham-Rugby in May, 1960.   *Photo by M. Mitchell*

ABOVE LEFT: Class J27 0-6-0 No. 65894 struggles past Londonderry Junction, Sunderland, with coal for the Newcastle area in January, 1967.　　*Photo by M. Dunnett*

BELOW LEFT: The road is cleared at Ryhope Colliery for the departure of Class J27 No. 65872 in October, 1966.　　*Photo by I. S. Carr*

RIGHT: Another J27, No. 65833, raises echoes at Felling, Gateshead, in September, 1966.
　　Photo by M. Dunnett

ABOVE LEFT: Class B1 4-6-0 No. 61296 leaves Wakefield with the Bradford portion of an express from Kings Cross in August, 1961.
Photo by G. W. Morrison

ABOVE RIGHT: Class WD 2-8-0s at Kings Cross shed in January, 1963.
Photo by D. L. Percival

BELOW LEFT: Class B1 4-6-0 No. 61115 passes Beeston with the 15.42 Leeds-Doncaster in August, 1962. *Photo by M. Mitchell*

BELOW RIGHT: Class B16/3 4-6-0 No. 61475 trundles a down GC line freight past Braunston & Willoughby in August, 1961.
Photo by M. Mitchell

A spread of Class Q6 0-8-0s—a pair meeting on Seaton Bank (ABOVE);
No. 63379 banking Consett coal past Annfield East in August, 1962
(ABOVE RIGHT); and No. 63445 drifting down from Annfield East
towards Stanley with coal for Tyneside.
Photos by I. S. Krause, J. M. Rayner, J. R. P. Hunt

Class A1 4-6-2 No. 60123 *H. A. Ivatt* sets out
from Leeds with the 17.10 Doncaster stopping
train in September, 1961. *Photo by J. M. Rayner*

The last years of British steam

4/Western Region

ABOVE: A Paddington-South
Wales express speeds downhill
through Wapley on the way
from Badminton to the Severn
Tunnel behind 4-6-0 No. 5093
Upton Castle in December, 1960.
Photo by G. F. Heiron

ABOVE: The up "Mayflower" from Plymouth to Paddington passes Dawlish behind 4-6-0 No. 6008 *King James II* in July, 1957.
Photo by T. K. Widd

BELOW: The 3.10 from Paddington arrives at Birmingham Snow Hill behind 4-6-0 No. 6005 *King George II* in September, 1962.
Photo by P. W. Simmonds

RIGHT: No. 6024 *King Edward I* rounds the bend on to the sea wall at Teignmouth with the 8.30 Plymouth-Paddington.
Photo by E. D. Bruton

ABOVE: A Plymouth-Penzance train between Saltash and St. Germains behind 4-6-0 No. 1006 *County of Cornwall* in April, 1949.

Photo by R. E. Vincent

LEFT: A "King" 4-6-0 leans to the curve past Dawlish Warren with the down "Cornish Riviera Express".

Photo by M. E. Ware

RIGHT: Another "County" 4-6-0, No. 1012 *County of Denbigh*, attacks the last stretch of Dainton Bank with westbound empty stock in September, 1955.

Photo by R. O. Tuck

LEFT: Class 6100 2-6-2T No. 6143 climbs towards Saunderton with a down local freight for Princes Risborough in April, 1964.   *Photo by Brian Stephenson*

ABOVE: Class 5101 2-6-2T No. 5154 approaches Kingham with an afternoon stopping train from Cheltenham St. James in August, 1962.   *Photo by M. Mensing*

BELOW: Another Class 5101 2-6-2T, No. 4125, enters Birmingham Snow Hill with the empty stock of an evening local to Leamington in June, 1964.   *Photo by R. W. Norfolk*

ABOVE: "Castle" class 4-6-0 No. 5060 *Earl of Berkeley* takes the Didcot avoiding line with a Sunday Paddington-Hereford express in February, 1957.   *Photo by T. E. Williams*

BELOW LEFT: Sister engine No. 5054 *Earl of Ducie* restarts the 12.05 Hereford-Paddington from Worcester Shrub Hill in June, 1964.   *Photo by B. J. Ashworth*

BELOW RIGHT: "Castle" Class 4-6-0 No. 5043 *Earl of Mount Edgecumbe* on the 9.45 Paddington-Worcester passes Class 7 4-6-2 No. 70028 *Royal Star* on the up "Capitals United Express" west of Twyford in February, 1959.

Photo by R. J. Blenkinsop

ABOVE: A summer Saturday Swindon-Penzance train climbs Dainton Bank doubleheaded by 4-6-0s Nos. 4950 *Patshull Hall* and 4991 *Cobham Hall* in August, 1957.
Photo by R. J. Blenkinsop

BELOW: A freight from the Midlands to London approaches West Ealing off the Greenford Loop behind 4-6-0 No. 6868 *Penrhos Grange* in November, 1963. *Photo by M. Pope*

RIGHT: Drifting through
Swindon shed yard is 4-6-0
No. 6862 *Derwent Grange*.

BELOW: A Paddington-bound
relief climbs Brewham Bank
near Bruton behind 4-6-0
No. 5992 *Horton Hall* in
September, 1962.
    Photo by G. A. Richardson

LEFT: Class 4300 2-6-0 No. 6317 banks a westbound freight to Whiteball Tunnel in March, 1951.
Photo by P. C. Short

BELOW LEFT: A Clarbeston Road-Fishguard Harbour local enters Fishguard & Goodwick station behind 2-6-0 No. 7318 in August, 1962.
Photo by E. Thomas

RIGHT: An afternoon Hereford-Gloucester train crosses the Wye at Backney behind a Class 4300 2-6-0 in October, 1964.
Photo by M. R. C. Price

BELOW RIGHT: Another 2-6-0, No. 5369, leaves Yeovil Pen Mill with the 16.28 Weymouth-Cardiff in August, 1961.
Photo by J. C. Haydon

LEFT: East of Stroud, 4-6-0 No. 5040 *Stokesay Castle* climbs through Chalford with an afternoon Cheltenham-Paddington express in May, 1955. *Photo by G. F. Heiron*

BELOW: On a frosty morning in November, 1965 4-6-0 No. 6956 *Mottram Hall* was photographed between Oxford and Radley with a London-bound freight. *Photo by J. A. M. Vaughan*

ABOVE LEFT: On the North-to-West route in July, 1963 2-8-2T No. 7220 heads towards Hereford with freight and is photographed south of Ludlow.   *Photo by J. R. Smith*

BELOW LEFT: An up freight of pit props on the South Wales main line near Rumney River Bridge Junction signalbox behind 2-8-0T No. 5202 in May, 1964.
    Photo by S. Rickard

ABOVE RIGHT: A freight emerges from the Severn Tunnel and approaches Pilning High Level in September, 1957 doubleheaded by 2-6-2T No. 3183 and 2-8-0 No. 2866.
    Photo by D. England

BELOW RIGHT: An up freight headed by 2-8-0 No. 4703 approaches Didcot in September, 1961.
    Photo by M. Mensing

ABOVE LEFT: Engine change at Bala, North Wales, in March, 1959: 0-6-0PT No. 7428 leaves its train to go on shed and be replaced by 0-6-0PT No. 8727.
Photo by G. W. Morrison

BELOW LEFT: An afternoon Pontypool Road train leaves Neath General in September, 1961 behind 0-6-2T No. 6652.
Photo by M. J. Fox

ABOVE RIGHT: A Banbury-Princes Risborough auto-train leaves Haddenham in March, 1954 behind 0-4-2T No. 1411.
Photo by J. F. Russell-Smith

BELOW RIGHT: Taking water at Tiverton Junction in August, 1964 is 0-4-2T No. 1450 preparatory to working a lunchtime auto-train to Tiverton.
Photo by I. G. Holt

LEFT: "Castle" 4-6-0 No. 5060 *Earl of Berkeley* passes Acocks Green with the Birmingham-Paddington "Inter-City" in April, 1962.

Photo by M. Mensing

RIGHT: The Paddington-Bristol "Merchant Venturer" hurries through Chippenham Junction in June, 1953 behind 4-6-0 No. 7024 *Powis Castle*.

Photo by G. F. Heiron

LEFT: "Star" class 4-6-0 No. 4036 *Queen Elizabeth* heads a Paddington-Plymouth relief near Hungerford on a July Saturday in 1951.
Photo by J. F. Russell-Smith

RIGHT: "Castle" class 4-6-0 No. 5083 *Bath Abbey* at Chipping Camden with the 12.55 Hereford-Paddington.
Photo by T. E. Williams

ABOVE LEFT: A West Drayton train leaves West Ealing in April, 1958 behind 0-6-0PT No. 9415.
Photo by K. L. Cook

ABOVE RIGHT: An evening Newport-Blaina train leaves Risca headed by 0-6-2T No. 6629 in June, 1960.
Photo by A. Smith

BELOW LEFT: On banking duty at Croes Newydd, Wrexham in November, 1965 is 0-6-2T No. 5677.
Photo by J. F. A. Hobbs

BELOW RIGHT: A down freight threads Birmingham Snow Hill station, headed by 0-6-0PT No. 5738, in September, 1953.
Photo by E. D. Bruton

BELOW: An Aberystwyth train at Oswestry in August, 1952 headed by "Dean Goods" 0-6-0 No. 2411; on the left 4-6-0 No. 7819 *Hinton Manor* waits to take over.   *Photo by B. E. Morrison*

ABOVE LEFT: An afternoon train to Pwllheli leaves Shrewsbury behind 4-6-0 No. 7802 *Bradley Manor*.   *Photo by B. E. Morrison*

BELOW RIGHT: "Dukedog" 4-4-0 No. 9004 pilots 2-6-0 No. 6340 through Central Wales near Glyndyfrdwy with the Saturday 7.20 Pwllheli-Paddington via Ruabon in August, 1959.   *Photo by L. N. Owen*

A "Manor" class 4-6-0 climbs through Cemmes Road with a Barmouth-Birmingham train on a summer Saturday in 1963.
Photo by M. Dunnett

RIGHT: The westbound "Cornish Riviera Express" near Twyford in February, 1955, headed by 4-6-0 No. 6024 *King Edward I.*   *Photo by T. E. Williams*

FAR RIGHT: The 14.35 Birkenhead-Paddington enters Birmingham Snow Hill in September, 1958 behind 4-6-0 No. 6000 *King George V.*   *Photo by M. Mensing*

BELOW LEFT: Double-chimney 4-6-0 No. 6026 *King John* assaults Hatton Bank with the 9.10 Paddington-Birkenhead in April, 1962.   *Photo by R. D. Timms*

BELOW RIGHT: "Britannia" 4-6-2 No. 70016 *Ariel* and 4-6-0 No. 6017 *King Edward IV* descend Hemerdon Bank towards Plympton with the 11.30 Paddington-Penzance in August, 1956.   *Photo by R. J. Blenkinsop*

ABOVE LEFT: A "Grange" 4-6-0 approaches Tramway Junction, Gloucester, with a freight from South Wales in September, 1964.
Photo by B. J. Ashworth

BELOW LEFT: Another "Grange", No. 6848 *Toddington Grange*, restarts a morning Evesham-Birmingham train from Stratford-upon-Avon in June, 1964. *Photo by T. E. Williams*

BELOW RIGHT: A summer Saturday Torquay-Paddington train enters Exeter St. Davids after a signal check outside the station behind 4-6-0 No. 4951 *Pendeford Hall* in August, 1965.
Photo by G. D. King

ABOVE LEFT: "Dukedog" 4-4-0 No. 9018 approaches Harlech with a Barmouth-Pwllheli train in May, 1955.   *Photo by P. H. Wells*

ABOVE RIGHT: A freight headed by 4-6-0 No. 6868 *Penrhos Grange* comes off the Greenford loop into West Ealing in November, 1963.   *Photo by M. Pope*

BELOW RIGHT: A morning train to Chester awaits departure from Oswestry behind 0-6-0 No. 2267 in September, 1956.   *Photo by P. J. Kelley*

ABOVE LEFT: A Gloucester-Worcester freight near Norton Halt behind 2-8-0 No. 3818 on a winter's day in January, 1963.
Photo by F. A. Haynes

BELOW LEFT: Another 2-8-0, No. 3858, climbs through Brimscombe, on the Swindon-Gloucester line, with a Reading-Severn Tunnel Junction freight in March, 1962.
Photo by G. T. Robinson

ABOVE RIGHT: Class "ROD" 2-8-0 No. 3020 heads freight near Stratford-upon-Avon in August, 1952.
Photo by B. England

BELOW RIGHT: Ready for work outside Cardiff Canton shed are 4-6-0s Nos. 1022 *County of Northampton* and 5970 *Hengrave Hall*.
Photo by G. F. Heiron

ABOVE LEFT: The Chalford auto-train trailer is sandwiched by 0-4-2T No. 1451 and 2-6-2T No. 5518 at Gloucester Central in March, 1964.

Photo by B. J. Ashworth

BELOW LEFT: A midday train for Paddington leaves Hereford in March, 1963 behind 4-6-0 No. 4916 *Crumlin Hall*.

Photo by A. A. Vickers

ABOVE RIGHT: On parcels van shunting duty at Birmingham Snow Hill in July, 1959 is 4-6-0 No. 7908 *Henshall Hall*.

Photo by M. Mensing

BELOW RIGHT: BR standard Class 4 4-6-0 No. 75008 approaches Severn Tunnel Junction with an afternoon Cardiff-Bristol train in 1958.

Photo by S. Rickard

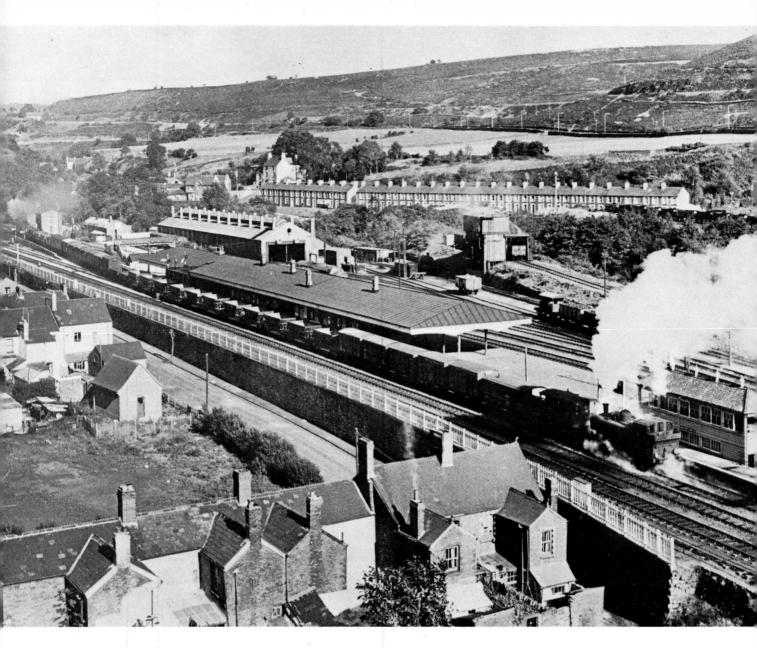

ABOVE: With 0-6-2T No. 5691 at the head and 0-6-0PT No. 9611 banking at the rear, a freight for the Merthyr line passes Abercynon in September, 1964.   *Photo by B. J. Ashworth*

BELOW LEFT: Ex-Rhymney Railway 0-6-2T No. 38 with a short Bargoed Pits freight on the Beddau loop in October, 1957.
Photo by S. Rickard

ABOVE RIGHT: An engineers' train returning from dismantling signal equipment between Brecon and Talybont crosses the Monmouthshire & Brecon Canal at Talybont in September, 1963.   *Photo by B. J. Ashworth*

BELOW: Class 4 2-6-4T No. 80096 pulls out of Barmouth with an evening train to Machynlleth in August, 1963.
   Photo by M. Dunnett

ABOVE LEFT: Running in after overhaul, 4-6-0 No. 2927 *Saint Patrick* heads a local out of Swindon.

BELOW LEFT: A returning summer Saturday St. Austell-Wolverhampton train passes Wilmcote behind 2-6-0 No. 5370 and 4-6-0 No. 7907 *Hart Hall* in August, 1958.

Photo by T. E. Williams

ABOVE: Restored to active life for a period, preserved 4-4-0 No. 3440 *City of Truro* heads a Birmingham-Reading and Swindon enthusiasts' special near Knowle & Dorridge in September, 1960.

Photo by M. Mensing

BELOW: An eastbound freight near Chipping Sodbury behind 4-6-0 No. 6961 *Stedham Hall* in May, 1963.

Photo by G. F. Heiron

LEFT: BR standard Class 4 4-6-0 No. 75033 clambers up to Talerddig Summit with the last up "Cambrian Coast Express" on March 4, 1967.
Photo by D. E. Gouldthorp

ABOVE: A special to the Talyllyn Railway is turned on the triangle at Morfa Mawddach by 4-6-0 No. 7827 *Lydham Manor* and 2-6-2T No. 4555 before the next stage of the journey to Towyn in September, 1964.
Photo by M. Pope

RIGHT: Evening at Barmouth in July, 1956, as the last auto-train of the day to Dolgelly crosses the Mawddach Estuary behind an 0-4-2T.
Photo by R. E. Vincent

ABOVE: A freight is restarted from a signal check at Shrewsbury by 4-6-0 No. 6849 *Walton Grange* in May, 1954.

Photo by C. G. Watford

RIGHT UPPER: Another "Grange", No. 6866 *Morfa Grange*, pilots 4-6-0 No. 4094 *Dynevor Castle* out of Stratford-upon-Avon with a Penzance-Wolverhampton train.

Photo by T. E. Williams

RIGHT LOWER: A Cinderford branch freight passes Soudley No. 1 ground frame behind 0-6-0PT No. 3681 in September, 1964.

Photo by B. J. Ashworth

LEFT UPPER: Conversation piece alongside 4-6-0 No. 1005 *County of Devon* at Chipping Sodbury in March, 1955.
Photo by G. F. Heiron

LEFT LOWER: "Britannia" Pacific No. 70029 *Shooting Star* gathers speed out of Cardiff past Pengam yards with the 7.50 Fishguard Harbour-Paddington in August, 1958.
Photo by G. F. Heiron

ABOVE RIGHT: A "Hall" 4-6-0 heads an eastbound express out of Newport across the River Usk.
Photo by G. F. Heiron

BELOW RIGHT: A trio of 2-8-0s, Nos. 2842, 2852 and 4701, is hauled to Sharpness Docks to be cut up by the branch passenger engine, 0-4-2T No. 1445, in July, 1964.
Photo by B. J. Ashworth

LEFT: An up freight trundles through Acocks Green, Birmingham, in November, 1958 behind 2-8-2T No. 7247.
Photo by M. Mensing

BELOW: A summer Saturday Churston-Paddington extra approaches Torquay in June, 1956 behind 2-8-0 No. 4702.

ABOVE: The 11.45 Bristol-Paddington non-stop speeds through Chipping Sodbury behind 4-6-0 No. 1023 *County of Oxford* in 1946.
Photo by G. F. Heiron

RIGHT: A combination of 4-6-0 6824 *Ashley Grange* and a "King" 4-6-0 storm Dainton Bank with a Plymouth-Paddington express.
Photo by M. E. Ware

The 8.55 Birkenhead-Paddington express emerges from
Harbury Tunnel behind 4-6-0 No. 6020 *King Henry IV* in
April, 1957.   *Photo by R. H. Short*

The last years of British steam

5/Southern Region

ABOVE: Class O2 0-4-4 No. W28 *Ashey* climbs out of Sandown with an afternoon train to Ventnor in June, 1964.
Photo by J. Goss

LEFT: "Merchant Navy" Pacific No. 35028 *Clan Line* pulls out of Southampton Central with the 12.10 Bournemouth-Waterloo in August, 1966; on the left "West Country" Pacific No. 34036 *Westward Ho* waits to follow with the 10.50 Weymouth-Waterloo.

Photo by B. J. Ashworth

RIGHT: "West Country" Pacific No. 34021 (originally named *Dartmoor*) heads past Clapham Junction to Waterloo in May, 1967.

Photo by P. Gerald

ABOVE: "Battle of Britain" Pacific No. 34071 *601 Squadron*
pauses at Farnborough in September, 1966.
Photo by J. H. Bird

LEFT: "Merchant Navy" Pacific No. 35001 *Channel Packet*
storms away from Worting Junction, Basingstoke, on the 10.30
Waterloo-Weymouth in August, 1964.
Photo by G. T. Robinson

ABOVE LEFT AND RIGHT: Class N15X 4-6-0 No. 32327
Trevithick heading the 18.09 Waterloo-Basingstoke in July, 1950,
overtakes a photographer in an electric train between Vauxhall
and Queen's Road.
Photos by C. C. B. Herbert

LEFT: Class H2 4-4-2 No. 32424 *Beachy Head* heads a down
Pullman special past Wandsworth Common in October, 1952.
Photo by E. R. Wethersett

LEFT UPPER: Class A1X 0-6-0T No. 32661 takes the timber viaduct across Langstone Harbour with a morning Havant-Hayling Island train in September, 1951. *Photo by P. M. Alexander*

BELOW LEFT: Class A1X 0-6-0Ts Nos. 32670 and 32636 pass Farlington Junction with empty stock from Fratton to Havant for a Hayling Island special trip in November, 1963.
Photo by S. C. Nash

ABOVE RIGHT: A pair of Class R1 0-6-0Ts climb out of Folkestone Harbour to Folkestone Central with one of the last steam-powered boat trains from the Channel port.
Photo by A. Ruddle

BELOW RIGHT: Another view of Langstone Bridge, on the Hayling Island branch, as a Class A1X 0-6-0T crosses in November, 1963.
Photo by R. A. Panting

ABOVE LEFT: "West Country" Pacific No. 34103 *Colstock* starts a midday boat train out of Victoria in January, 1958.
Photo by D. Herman

BELOW LEFT: "Battle of Britain" Pacific No. 34066 *Spitfire* tops Blacksole Summit, near Herne Bay, with the down Kentish Belle.
Photo by P. Ransome-Wallis

BELOW RIGHT: "Merchant Navy" Pacific No. 35026 *Lamport & Holt Line* threads Ashford station with a midday down boat train, passing Class E 4-4-0 No. 31514 on the right in March, 1953.
Photo by D. Cross

ABOVE: "Schools" 4-4-0 No. 30913 *Christ's Hospital* tackles Sole Street Bank with a Ramsgate-Victoria train in June, 1955.
Photo by S. Creer

ABOVE LEFT: Class N 2-6-0 No. 31866 leaves Crowthorne with the 15.55 Reading-Redhill in October, 1964.
Photo by G. T. Robinson

ABOVE RIGHT: Class W 2-6-4T No. 31920 winds a freight off the West London extension line through Clapham Junction en route from Willesden Junction to Norwood Yard in November, 1962.
Photo by B. Stephenson

BELOW LEFT: Class U 2-6-0 No. 31790 heads the 12.35 Reading out of Redhill in January, 1965.
Photo by G. D. King

BELOW RIGHT: A pair of Class W 2-6-4Ts, Nos. 31914 and 31924, pause at Exeter Central in August, 1963 between banking jobs up from Exeter St. Davids; on the left "West Country" Pacific No. 34002 *Salisbury* waits to leave with the 11.28 to Ilfracombe.
Photo by David Hill

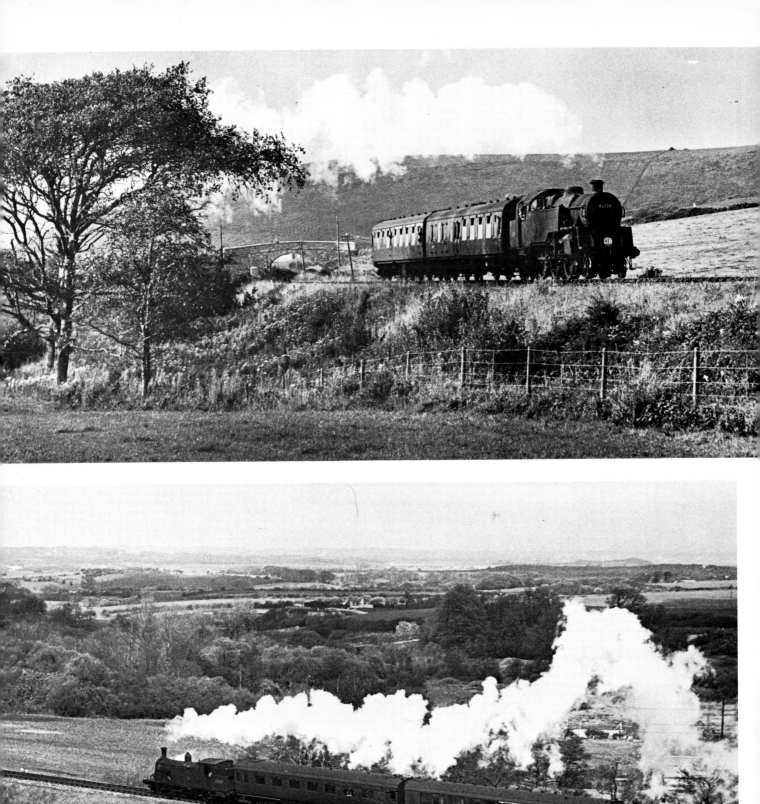
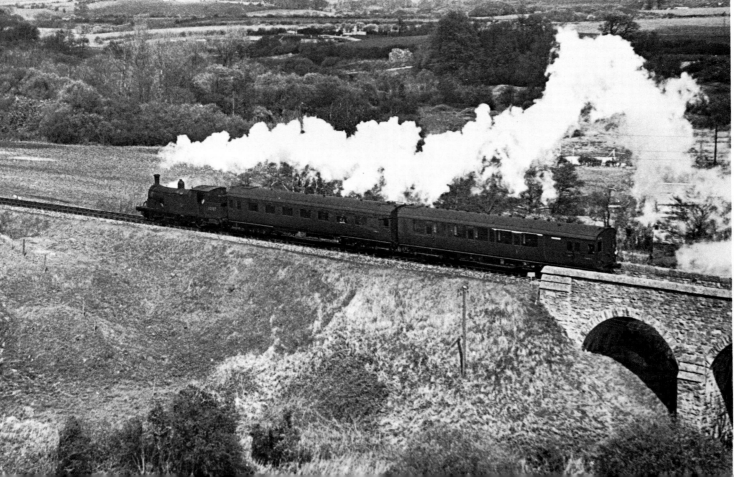

ABOVE LEFT: An afternoon Wareham-Swanage train near Corfe Castle behind Class 4 2-6-4T No. 80138 in August, 1966.
Photo by L. A. Nixon

ABOVE RIGHT: Class 0298 2-4-0WT No. 30585 takes water in Dunmere Wood with a Wenford Bridge branch freight in Cornwall in April, 1960.
Photo by N. M. Lera

BELOW LEFT: Class M7 0-4-4T No. 30107 pulls out of Corfe Castle with the 13.40 Swanage-Wareham in April, 1964.
Photo by R. A. Panting

BELOW RIGHT: Another view of Corfe Castle as the 16.20 from Swanage departs for Wareham behind tender-first Class 4 4-6-0 No. 75065 in May, 1966.
Photo by J. H. Bird

TOP: Class H15 4-6-0 No. 30489 dips under the Battledown flyover, near Basingstoke, on a summer Saturday Waterloo-West Country relief in June, 1951
Photo by P. M. Alexander

CENTRE: Class L12 4-4-0 No. 30427 mounts Battledown flyover with a summer Saturday Portsmouth-Midlands extra in August, 1951.
Photo by E. D. Bruton

BOTTOM: Class S15 4-6-0 No. 30511 takes the Bournemouth line from Worting Junction, Basingstoke with a down freight.
Photo by B. H. Kimber

ABOVE: Class S15 4-6-0 No. 30833 heads under the Battledown flyover towards Salisbury in October, 1964.
Photo by M. Pope

BELOW: Another Battledown flyover view, with Class N15 4-6-0 No. 30783 *Sir Gillemere* heading a Salisbury-Waterloo semi-fast.
Photo by D. Cross

ABOVE LEFT: Class H 0-4-4T No. 31500 moves the 9.58 Tunbridge-Maidstone West out of Paddock Wood in March, 1961.
Photo by M. Pope

BELOW LEFT: Another Class H, No. 31520, works the empty stock of an Allhallows-on-Sea excursion past Sharnal Street back to Gravesend.
Photo by D. Cross

RIGHT: The 13.08 from Three Bridges to East Grinstead soon after departure in February, 1960 behind Class H 0-4-4T No. 31530.
Photo by J. C. Beckett

ABOVE: "Merchant Navy" Pacific No. 35003 *Royal Mail* attacks Semley Bank with an Exeter-Waterloo express in August, 1960.
Photo by G. A. Richardson

BELOW: A Waterloo-Southampton Docks boat train in the last days of steam haulage on this main line passes Vauxhall soon after leaving London behind Class 4 4-6-0 No. 75074 in February, 1967.
Photo by J. Seddon

ABOVE LEFT: Class E4 0-6-2T No. 32581 on Forest Row bank with the 17.14 Tunbridge Wells West-East Croydon via East Grinstead in August, 1951.
Photo by S. C. Nash

ABOVE RIGHT: Another E4, No. 32468, approaches Goring-by-Sea with a short freight in June, 1962.
Photo by A. A. Vickers

BELOW LEFT: Class A1X 0-6-0T No. 32636 and Class E6 0-6-2T No. 32418 move a special out of Lewes towards Seaford in October, 1962.
Photo by A. R. Butcher

LOWER RIGHT: Class 13 4-4-2T No. 32082 approaches Clapham Junction with the 11.08 Victoria-Oxted in July, 1949.
Photo by C. C. B. Herbert

ABOVE LEFT: Class 700 0-6-0 No. 30316 on a breakdown train near Eastleigh in September, 1955.
Photo by L. Elsey

ABOVE RIGHT: Class C 0-6-0 No. 31588 passes Grove Junction, Tunbridge Wells, with the 15.18 Tunbridge Wells Central-Hastings in February, 1960.
Photo by M. J. Esau

BELOW LEFT: Class Q 0-6-0 No. 30530 near Billingshurst, heading a special between Horsham and Midhurst in October, 1964.
Photo by B. Stephenson

BELOW RIGHT: Class C 0-6-0 No. 31268 pulls out of Adisham with a Faversham-Dover train in June, 1959.
Photo by P. Ransome-Wallis

RIGHT: Class N15 4-6-0 No. 30768 *Sir Balin* makes for the
Kent coast with a Victoria-Ramsgate express in the summer of 1957.
Photo by P. Ransome-Wallis

BELOW LEFT: An Exeter-Waterloo express passes Yeovil
Junction behind Class N15 4-6-0 No. 30453 *King Arthur*.

BELOW RIGHT: Class D1 4-4-0 No. 31489 double-heads
"Schools" Class 4-4-0 No. 30935 *Sevenoaks* past Weald Box
with a midday Charing Cross-Ramsgate train.
Photo by Derek Cross.

The Adams 4-4-2Ts of Class 0415.

ABOVE LEFT: No. 30583 shunting a Waterloo-Lyme Regis through coach at Axminster in August, 1954.

ABOVE RIGHT: No. 30582 approaching Virginia Water with an enthusiasts' special in March, 1961.

BELOW LEFT: No. 30582 near the end of its career on the Lyme Regis branch, climbing from Axminster to Combpyne in October, 1960.

BELOW RIGHT: Another Lyme Regis branch scene, with No. 30583 about to cross Cannington Viaduct in June, 1959.

Photos by J. Robertson,
J. C. Beckett, C. P. Boocock,
J. H. Aston

ABOVE LEFT: Class 4 2-6-0 No. 76029 pulls out of Southampton Terminus with a Bournemouth train in August, 1955.
Photo by T. G. Cleare

BELOW LEFT: Class L 4-4-0 No. 31771 leaves Tunbridge with empty stock.
Photo by Derek Cross

ABOVE RIGHT: Class D 4-4-0 No. 31737 moves a hop pickers' special out of Paddock Wood in September, 1955.
Photo by S. C. Nash

BELOW RIGHT: Class 5 4-6-0 No. 73020 hurries the 13.30 Waterloo-Weymouth through Walton-on-Thames in 1967.
Photo by J. H. Bird

ABOVE LEFT: Class Q1 0-6-0s Nos. 33027 and 33006 leave Baynards for Guildford with an enthusiasts' special in June, 1965.

ABOVE RIGHT: Class 0395 0-6-0 No. 30580 pilots Class N 2-6-0 No. 31864 out of Guildford with freight in the Aldershot direction in June, 1949.
Photo by P. M. Alexander

BELOW LEFT: A down track train south of Gatwick Airport in July, 1961 is headed by Class K 2-6-0 No. 32352.
Photo by J. C. Beckett

BELOW RIGHT: Class C2X 0-6-0 No. 32434 arriving from East Grinstead is seen through the departure signals at the east end of Lewes station in August, 1956.
Photo by F. J. Saunders

ABOVE LEFT: "Merchant Navy" Pacif[ic] No. 35030 *Elder-Dempster Lines* ploughs through the rain into Surbiton with the down "Bournemouth Belle" in April, 196[ ]
Photo by J. H. Cooper-Smith

BELOW LEFT: Here the down "Bournemouth Belle" passing Durnsfor[d] Road Power Station, Wimbledon, in November, 1964, is headed by a "West Country" Class Pacific No. 34002 *Salisbu[ry]*
Photo by B. Stephenson

ABOVE RIGHT: Rebuilt "West Country" Pacific No. 31407 *Ilfracombe* takes water at Alton, diverted from its normal route with the down "Bournemouth Belle" in April, 1966 because of pre-electrification works.
Photo by M. Pope

BELOW RIGHT: Rebuilt "Battle of Britain" Pacific No. 34056 *Croydon* pulls out of Exeter Central with a Waterloo-bound section of the "Atlantic Coast Express".
Photo by J. B. Wells

ABOVE LEFT: Class H15 4-6-0 No. 30476 passes Cosham with a Chichester-Salisbury freight in November, 1951.
Photo by P. M. Alexander

BELOW LEFT: Class T9 4-4-0 No. 30338 coasts into Padstow with a train from Wadebridge in June, 1960.
Photo by K. R. Pirt

ABOVE RIGHT: Class T9 4-4-0 No. 30286 near Stockbridge with a Portsmouth-Andover train in November, 1957.
Photo by S. C. Nash

BELOW RIGHT: A Seaton branch train near Colyford in September, 1961 behind Class M7 0-4-4T No. 30667.
Photo by M. J. Esau

ABOVE LEFT: Study of Class M7
0-4-4T No. 30213 on carriage pilot duty at
Clapham Junction in April, 1949.
Photo by C. C. B. Herbert

BELOW LEFT: BR standard Class 4
2-6-4T No. 80089 leaves Redhill with the
7.27 to Eastbourne, Tonbridge and
Eridge in August, 1964.
Photo by G. D. King

ABOVE RIGHT: Action study of Class USA 0-6-0T No. 30064 on enthusiasts' special duty in October, 1964.

Photo by M. Pope

BELOW RIGHT: Class M7 0-4-4T No. 30108 at Brockenhurst with a Ringwood line train.

Photo by B. H. Kimber

ABOVE LEFT: Class H15 4-6-0 No. 30486 about to leave Waterloo with a Southampton Docks boat train in July, 1953.

Photo by J. N. Faulkner

RIGHT: Class U 2-6-0 No. 31795 clambers up the 1 in 80 gradient between Rowlands Castle and the South Downs summit near Petersfield with a Portsmouth-Nine Elms freight in November, 1951.

Photo by P. M. Alexander

ABOVE CENTRE: The fireman of Class D15 4-4-0 No. 30467 picks up the staff for the single line at Fareham on a Sunday afternoon train from Portsmouth to Eastleigh in 1949.

Photo by P. C. Short

BELOW LEFT: Triple-header on an August Saturday morning Exeter-Ilfracombe train in August, 1955—Class N 2-6-0s Nos. 31845 and 31846 sandwich "West Country" Pacific No. 34035 *Shaftesbury*.

Photo by P. W. Gray

ABOVE LEFT: Class U 2-6-0 No. 31804 and Class N15 4-6-0 No. 30454 *Queen Guinevere* alongside the Salisbury coaling stage in March, 1959.
Photo by Ivo Peters

BELOW LEFT: Rebuilt "West Country" Pacific No. 34005 *Barnstable* between Gillingham and Templecombe with a Waterloo-Exeter express in September, 1963.
Photo by A. Richardson

ABOVE RIGHT: Rebuilt "Battle of Britain" Pacific No. 34056 *Croydon* at Yeovil Pen Mill in May, 1964, about to set off for Yeovil Town with the empty stock of a Whit-Monday relief from Weymouth.

Photo by W. G. Sumner

BELOW RIGHT: "Lord Nelson" Class 4-6-0 No. 30863 *Lord Rodney* approaches Millbrook, Southampton, with the 10.50 from Hinton Admiral to Waterloo in July, 1960.

Photo by R. A. Panting

Bulleid Pacifics as built and rebuilt.
ABOVE: In its original form, "Merchant Navy" No. 35029 *Ellerman Lines* climbs near Knockholt with a Victoria-Dover boat train.

BELOW: Rebuilt "West Country" No. 34013 *Okehampton* emerges from Buckhorn Weston tunnel with the up "Atlantic Coast Express" in September, 1963.
Photo by A. Richardson

ABOVE RIGHT: Class S15 4-6-0 No. 30511 pulls out of Lyndhurst Road with a Southampton Terminus-Wimborne train in June, 1963.
Photo by M. J. Fox

BELOW RIGHT: Class C2X 0-6-0 No. 32540 leaves Brighton for Newhaven with the empty LMR stock of a Lourdes boat special in May, 1954.
Photo by J. H. W. Kent

ABOVE: Class B4 0-4-0T No. 30084 shunts the Eastern Docks at Dover.
Photo by P. Ransome-Wallis

RIGHT: A Reading-Redhill train approaches Shalford behind Class E 4-4-0 No. 31516.
Photo by E. Griffiths

BELOW: "Schools" Class 4-4-0 No. 30932 *Blundells* climbs past Petts Wood Junction with a down Eastern Section express in the summer of 1954.
Photo by R. Russell

ABOVE LEFT: Isle of Wight Class O2 0-4-4Ts Nos. W20 *Shanklin* and W16 *Ventnor* double-head the 7.40 Ryde Pier-Ventnor train near Brading in July, 1965.

Photo by P. J. Russell

BELOW LEFT: Isle of Wight trains, each headed by a Class O2 0-5-4T, pass at Smallbrook Junction in June, 1966; the down train for Shanklin is waiting for the up train in the foreground to come off the single line from Brading.

Photo by G. D. King

BELOW RIGHT: Another Class O2, No. W22 *Brading*, nears Wroxall with the 17.40 Ventnor-Ryde Pierhead in July, 1965.

Photo by P. J. Russell

ABOVE: An Isle of Wight Class O2 0-4-4T heads for Ryde from the Pierh with an evening train to Ventnor in August, 1965.

Photo by V. Wake

BELOW LEFT: Class O2 No. 35 *Freshwater* has its smokebox cleared a Ventnor after arrival from Ryde Pierh in July, 1965.

Photo by P. J. Russell